Blastoff! Beginners are developed by literacy experts and educators to meet the needs of early readers. These engaging informational texts support young children as they begin reading about their world. Through simple language and high frequency words paired with crisp, colorful photos, Blastoff! Beginners launch young readers into the universe of independent reading.

Sight Words in This Book

a	eat	is	some	under
an	find	like	that	what
and	for	look	their	white
at	go	make	they	
away	have	must	this	
black	her	run	to	

This edition first published in 2022 by Bellwether Media, Inc.

No part of this publication may be reproduced in whole or in part without written permission of the publisher. For information regarding permission, write to Bellwether Media, Inc., Attention: Permissions Department, 6012 Blue Circle Drive, Minnetonka, MN 55343.

Library of Congress Cataloging-in-Publication Data

Names: McDonald, Amy, author.
Title: Skunks / Amy McDonald.
Description: Minneapolis, MN : Bellwether Media, 2022. | Series: Blastoff! beginners : Animals in my yard | Includes bibliographical references and index. | Audience: Ages 4-7 | Audience: Grades K-1
Identifiers: LCCN 2021000774 (print) | LCCN 2021000775 (ebook) | ISBN 9781644874752 (library binding) | ISBN 9781648343834 (ebook)
Subjects: LCSH: Skunks--Juvenile literature.
Classification: LCC QL737.C248 M425 2022 (print) | LCC QL737.C248 (ebook) | DDC 599.76/8--dc23
LC record available at https://lccn.loc.gov/2021000774
LC ebook record available at https://lccn.loc.gov/2021000775

Text copyright © 2022 by Bellwether Media, Inc. BLASTOFF! BEGINNERS and associated logos are trademarks and/or registered trademarks of Bellwether Media, Inc.

Editor: Christina Leaf   Designer: Brittany McIntosh

Printed in the United States of America, North Mankato, MN.

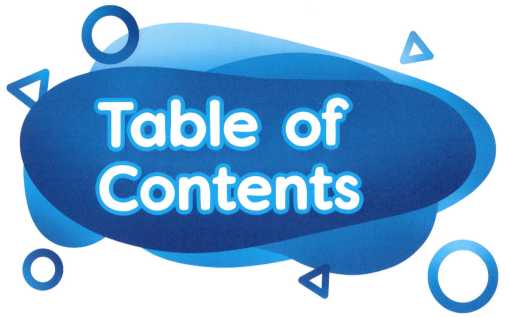

Table of Contents

Skunks!	4
Body Parts	6
The Lives of Skunks	10
Skunk Facts	22
Glossary	23
To Learn More	24
Index	24

Skunks!

What is that smell? Hello, skunk!

Body Parts

Skunks have black and white fur. They have fluffy tails.

fur

Skunks have **glands** under their tails. They stink!

The Lives of Skunks

Skunks live alone. They make **dens** for homes.

den

Skunks find food
at night.
They eat plants,
mice, and bugs.

plants

mice

bugs

13

This skunk brings an apple to her **kit**.

Skunks look like food to some animals. They must keep safe.

Skunks hiss and stamp their feet. This means go away!

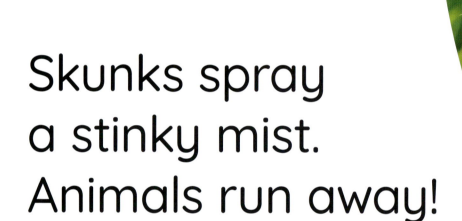

Skunks spray
a stinky mist.
Animals run away!

Skunk Facts

Skunk Body Parts

fur

tail

glands

Skunk Food

plants   mice   bugs

Glossary

dens

homes built by animals

glands

body parts that let out a smelly spray

kit

a baby skunk

To Learn More

ON THE WEB

FACTSURFER

Factsurfer.com gives you a safe, fun way to find more information.

1. Go to www.factsurfer.com.

2. Enter "skunks" into the search box and click 🔍.

3. Select your book cover to see a list of related content.

Index

animals, 16, 20
apple, 14
bugs, 12, 13
dens, 10
feet, 18
food, 12, 16
fur, 6
glands, 8
hiss, 18

homes, 10
kit, 14, 15
mice, 12, 13
night, 12
plants, 12
smell, 4
spray, 20
stamp, 18
stink, 8, 20

tails, 6, 7, 8

The images in this book are reproduced through the courtesy of: Eric Isselee, front cover, pp. 3, 7, 9, 22 (top); mauritius images GmbH/ Alamy, p. 5; Holly Kuchera, p. 6; critterbiz, pp. 10, 23 (kit); Sumbul, p. 10; LianeM, p. 12; Gina Kelly/ Alamy, p. 13 (top); Rudmer Zwerver, p. 13 (bottom left); Daniel Prudek, p. 13 (bottom right); Geoffrey Kuchera, pp. 15, 17; Mircea Costina, p. 19; Jim Cumming, p. 20; Don Johnston_MA/ Alamy, p. 21; Ernstafan, p. 22 (plants); jitkagold, p. 22 (mice); S.O.E, p. 22 (bugs); A_Lesik, p. 23 (dens); Ultrashock, p. 23 (glands).

24